THE LITTLE BOOK OF
WORSHIP LEADING

Everything I wish I knew when I started out

by Angie Lendon

The Little Book of Worship Leading

Copyright 2018 Angie Lendon
All rights reserved

ISBN-13: 978-1720819400
ISBN-10: 1720819408

No part of this book may be used or reproduced in any manner without written permission of the author. This book may not be reprinted without permission from the author.

Published by Angie Lendon

Book design & formatting by Laura Murray at Peanut Designs www.pnutd.co.uk

DEDICATION

To my grandchildren Evie and Lily and those yet to come. Let this book encourage you that learning is a lifelong thing and not just what you achieve in school! May you always make life work for you and not work for life! You are loved and celebrated!

ACKNOWLEDGEMENTS

Nigel my rock and biggest supporter

Tim, Anna, Dan, and Hanna my kids and in laws who make me proud to be their mum and are my biggest achievement.

Evie Jemima and Lily Rae my gorgeous granddaughters who have enhanced my life and caused my heart to love in a way I didn't know I could!

Andrew and Laura Murray for "getting me" being the door opener that you've been and for your willingness to undertake all things design!

Maggie Carr for editing, proof reading and coffee dates that spurred me on!

Joanne Milnes for making sure I come aside and keep it real

Jarrod and Vicky Cooper and the Revive Church family who run with passion and release me to make an impact for the Kingdom!

Chris Bowater and Dave Hadden for being my "dad" and walking me through some challenging places whilst bringing wisdom and laughter in abundance!

CONTENTS

INTRODUCTION

1. THE AUTHENTICITY OF WORSHIP
2. WHO ARE YOU?
3. RIVER OR CANAL
4. SONGS FOR THE JORNEY
5. THE PROPHETIC SONG
6. DEAR FRIEND

INTRODUCTION

The growth and influence of worship ministry in the U.K. in the last 25 years has been phenomenal. When I moved to the U.K. from America in 1991 there was very little in the way of recorded worship or contemporary Christian music available to purchase. Today we are spoiled for choice with many genres available.

My own journey has certainly been influenced by those who have pioneered the way. The likes of Chris Bowater, Dave Hadden Darlene Zschech and more recently Brian and Jen Johnson, Jesus Culture and Kimberly and Alberto Rivera who have significantly contributed to the freedom of expression we have in worship today.

I am a firm believer of sharing lessons learned to the rising generations of worship leaders. There are many things that I wished I'd known when I was starting out. Sure there were books by high profile worship ministries but I needed the nuts and bolts. Some things are caught but so much has to be taught. I wandered around trying to figure stuff out like what was the Song of the Lord? If I sang it how did I know it was coming from God and not me? Was I good enough to sing on His behalf? Could I backtrack to a previous song if I'd moved on too quickly? How could I pitch a song so that I could sing it without excluding the congregation? These questions and more needed answers and as I wasn't a musician and didn't have lots of musical knowledge I felt a fake!

Thus began a journey of pioneering the way of leading worship with my voice as the instrument. It took time, patience and great investment in relationships and forging ways to communicate musically with a voice! There were times where I'd get off that platform, run to the toilet and cry, feeling like I'd messed it up, but there were many more times where we would hit the sweet spot and something incredible would happen as the tangible presence of God invaded those meetings. There have been heart lessons to learn, arrogance to tame and identity and confidence to be found on this incredible journey!

It is my hope that this little book of worship leading will open up the horizons for those just getting started as well as those who have been in the ministry for a while. It's good to go back to basics every now and then. I sincerely pray you enjoy reading and answering the questions with your worship teams as much as I did in the preparation and writing.

YOU KNOW EVERYTHING ABOUT ME, WHEN I SIT AND WHEN I RISE

You know everything about me, when I sit and when I rise

1
THE AUTHENTICITY OF WORSHIP

The dictionary describes Authentic as - the undisputed origin and not a copy; It is genuine. Brene Brown says "Authenticity is a collection of choices that we have to make every day. It's about the choice to show up and be real. The choice to be honest. The choice to let out true selves be seen."

We live in a comparison driven culture and I think one of the greatest challenges the church faces today is that of authenticity.

We are inundated with high profile mega churches and movements via social networking and whilst this opens up new songs to us it also brings a greater temptation to copy what we see and hear.

We are created as originals, a blank page for God to write on. Our churches have a particular DNA that God breathed into life at its conception.

There is a sound for your house that will resonate with the mandate that God has given your leadership in order to reach the people in your community.

Recently God showed me a picture of a huge library in heaven that had volumes and volumes of songs. These volumes were covered in dust. On the cover was printed the names of different churches across the earth. But no one was using them. The volumes that were not dusty had the names of well-known churches printed on them. Hillsong, Jesus Culture, Bethel, Elevation, House-fires and others. The skins on these volumes were well worn. I saw God pushing the dusty volumes towards seeking hands of worship and church leaders looking for songs but they kept pushing them back and reaching for the known song books!

What would it look like if we got before God and with sincere hearts asked Him to download the songs for our people, our churches and our communities?

I believe that every church has a unique sound and frequency that, like DNA cannot be reproduced by any other church. We will look at this in a later chapter.

Bethel, Hillsong and other high profile worship movements are so successful because they have discovered their sound of worship and it has drawn people to find Jesus.

When we discover our sound I believe we will experience the same.

"But I can't write songs Angie" I hear you say. "I wasn't born with that gift" I used to say the same thing. I thought people were born songwriters and you just had this amazing gift. Yet God had songs waiting for me to write. When I partnered with Him and allowed Him to show me and download to me the songs in Heaven I started to write and went on to record 2 albums. I didn't even know what chords were when I started". I used to write the 3 notes that I played on the piano and record myself singing then give it to a musician to figure out!

If you will just take what's in your hands and give it to God He will multiply it and grow your skills.

One of the greatest lessons I've learned is how Holy Spirit will step in where we finish and I don't need to strive as He is so capable of filling the gaps. When I started leading worship and playing keys for myself He would step in and fill in the gaps. Sometimes I'd hear notes being played that were nowhere near my fingers!!

I want to encourage you to seek after God and ask Him to lead you to the songs He has waiting that will bring the lost into your church.

Look beyond your immediate team too. There could be someone in your church who has heard God and has a lyric or a phrase that is like a clue to finding the song. It's time to think outside of the box!

One of the songs on my album From Hull with Love called Wake Up! Was birthed by someone in our congregation who gave me a few lines and it sparked the rest of the song. There might be something spoken in a meeting that Holy Spirit breathes on and we can catch this and write it into a song that will bring breakthrough.

I recently heard a quote from Edward Young who said "we are all born originals why is it so many of us die copies?"

Let's not be one of those people. Let's leave a creative footprint of heaven in our churches and communities that will lead people to Jesus.

POINTS TO PONDER

• How do you keep the authenticity in your worship leading and playing/singing?

• How confident are you in your identity and calling?

• Do you find yourself measuring and comparing your abilities against other people on your team?

I HAVE COME TO BE HONEST WITH YOU

2
WHO ARE YOU?

Perhaps the greatest battle we have as believers is that of identity.

I love this fab quote "People of real humility have a lot of confidence in who God is inside them. They have submitted to His leadership and steward the confidence they have gained through personal process. They don't hate who they are but say "yes and amen" to who God made them to be. They are grateful that God operates within them and they don't need to flaunt anything to get validation." Mark DeJesus

Joyce Meyer in her book Battlefield for the Mind writes "Stop determining your worth and value by what other people say. Be determined by what the Word of God says."

So often we allow other people to define us by their words. That old poem about sticks and stones and calling names not hurting is untrue! All of these things can and will hurt us if we allow them to penetrate into our hearts and our minds. We begin to believe the lies and when we enter into agreement with them we start to live them out but the bible is crammed full of scriptures that describe and affirm our identity!

John 1:12, "Yet to all who did receive him, to those who believed in his name, he gave the right to become children of God"
Ephesians 1:5 "he predestined us for adoption to sonship through Jesus Christ, in accordance with his pleasure and will"

1 Peter 2:9 "But you are a chosen people, a royal priesthood, a holy nation, God's special possession, that you may declare the praises of him who called you out of darkness into his wonderful light"

As worship ministries and creatives we have a sensitivity that is part of our "wiring" we need this in order to minister in the way that we do, to hear Holy Spirit and follow His leading.

However when this sensitivity gets out of balance we can find ourselves taking things the wrong way allowing the lies of the enemy to distort our thinking.

Worship is the number one thing the devil sets out to destroy! Why? Because worship ushers us into the presence of God and brings freedom, joy, healing and deliverance. Satan loses his grip on us and he knows we are then released to have a full revelation of God and expand the kingdom of heaven.

You will know that Satan held some form of position in heaven (some believe one of worship) until pride, arrogance, and ambition took a greater hold on his heart and we know the end of the story. He along with thousands of angels were cast out of heaven.

If we don't have a firm grasp on the truth of our identity in Christ these same character flaws can rear their heads in us at any given time. We are not immune from them. We can become competitive, insecure, and threatened by another's gift. We can even become paranoid that no one likes us, and that we're not accepted which then causes us to separate ourselves from others as we withdraw. There is a danger in this.

Let's look at the account of the Danites in Judges 19. They were looking for a place to settle and sent out 5 men to explore the area. The men found Laish which was a quiet and secure community. They attacked them and burned their city to the ground. The bible says "there was no one to deliver them because they were far away from Sidon and they had no ties with anyone"

Their independence and lack of relationship made them vulnerable and they perished. I've observed too often, people walking away and separating from the church and relationships. They end up far away from God and it's hard to watch them needlessly struggle.

Psalm 139 says "we are fearfully and wonderfully made." Just stop for a minute and reflect on that phrase. Savour each word and let it sink in. When Jesus looks at us He sees no flaws, no bad, no negative, and no weakness. We cannot change that. It's non-negotiable. What He says goes!

Ephesians 2:10 tells us "we are God's masterpiece" A masterpiece is described in the dictionary as "a work of outstanding artistry, skill, or workmanship.
"A great literary masterpiece"
It is described as a triumph, a coup, and marvellous feat, a feather in one's cap, wonder, sensation, outstanding example, paragon, great work, showpiece, gem, and prize.

This description certainly doesn't sound like something of low value! Yet Jesus says we are his masterpiece but we disagree?

If I'm honest I'm not very good at receiving compliments. I often answer with a justification of why I'm receiving that compliment instead of responding with a smile and a thank you!

This is what we do with Jesus. The justification has already been established at the cross of Calvary! We have no need to justify His love and acceptance of us.

Jesus vision of us is seen through the red lens of His blood. He will take us where we are and call us into who He sees. God met Gideon hiding at the threshing floor and called him a mighty warrior! Everything about Gideon was so un-warrior like in that instance but it made no difference to Gods identity bestowed upon him. Jesus changed Peter's name after he had the revelation of who Christ was! He went from being a big mouth, putting his foot in it and messing up big time to the rock upon which the church was built! Jacob had a revelation of the presence of God at Bethel and God changed his name to Israel! Can you see how the revelation of who God is and who we are in Him is so pivotal in our moving forward into the call and destiny God has called us into? This is why Satan does his utmost to cripple us with his lies!

Make it a priority to regularly read the word and declare it over yourself. Take those thoughts captive when they come. We have to be active not passive in our response to this very real threat to our identity. We are in a battle. It's a constant battle so we must be constant in our pursuit of the word of God in our lives. As we would dress ourselves with clothing to keep warm and protected from the natural elements so we must clothe ourselves in the spiritual armour of truth as described in Ephesians 6.

POINTS TO PONDER

- Do you sometimes find it hard to see yourself as God sees you like Gideon did?

- What part of the armour of God do you need most right now? Why?

- Write out Psalm 139:14 and meditate on it. Ask Holy Spirit to give you fresh revelation.

3
RIVER OR CANAL?

Revelation 22:1 "Then he showed me a river of the water of life, clear as crystal, coming from the throne of God and of the Lamb,"
Psalm 46:4 "There is a river whose streams make glad the city of God, The holy dwelling places of the Most High."

As worshippers we are invited to get into the river and follow the presence of God that flows from His throne. Let's take a brief look at rivers and canals.

We know that a river starts out as a stream in a high place and that as it runs down the mountain or hillside other streams merge with it, forming a larger body of water which we know as the river.

Rivers flow with a reasonable amount of power and they carve out and shape the land as they move through it. Sometimes rivers double back on themselves and so they revisit the same scenery but from a different vantage point.

Canals are man-made to provide a means of transport to get from A to B in the quickest time possible. They are rigid and are not subject to the elements like a river is. Canals are used to link places together.

When we lead worship we want to be following the river

Canal worship has a set list of songs and works down these songs until it is complete. I don't have a problem with set lists. They are good to use as a place to launch from. However, I never want to be bound by that list. I want to be able to deviate from it if the Holy Spirit wants to take the worship in a different direction. Bob Sorge in his book "Following the River" suggests that if we're going to use the canal style of worship that we do so with a CD.

I've always wanted to take a holiday on a river boat. There is so much to be seen and it is an adventure in the making. So it is with river worship. We have a starting place, but we're never quite sure where we will end up and what we will see along the way. Sometimes we double back on ourselves and revisit from that different perspective, and there are times when we catch a current that propels us along with little effort.

River worship can sometimes be scary because we are truly letting go and allowing Holy Spirit to take the lead. We give him the rudder and we go where he wants to go. We relinquish control and we don't really know what's going to happen. But this is the great part of the adventure of worship. We follow the fresh flow and we catch the rapids and it is fun! It's safe because Holy Spirit is safe. I cannot tell you the amount of times I've found myself in a meeting thinking "I have no idea what to do now!" Working with a meeting host can be of great value in this situation as you can share the responsibility and it alleviates any pressure we may feel. Sometimes there's nothing to be done and we must learn to linger and not always jump in to the next song or even to say something. There are times where God is just wanting to connect with each person individually in a corporate setting. I want to encourage you not to be afraid of space and silence.

I remember being in a meeting where it felt like we were trying to sail through treacle! It was hard work. We were going through songs one after the other and you could feel the atmosphere getting more and more stifled. We were trying our best to lead the people but something needed to break. I remember asking to the Lord "What's happening? Why is it so hard? Why doesn't someone do something?" He replied "I'm waiting for YOU to do something!" With that He gave me a clear instruction to create space and allow for him to breathe on us. We let a simple chord hang and at first it was squirmy and uncomfortable but one by one people began to lift their voices and worshipped with their song instead of the song on the screen and a sound was released that caused a man to be healed of a serious medical condition and another to encounter the Father heart of God in a very deep way.

It's so easy for us to close our eyes and be in our moment or just plain scared that we fail to look at the congregation and evaluate where they are at on this worship journey. The very people we are leading are often the clues the Holy Spirit will use to lead us to the place He wants to go. It's good practice to have a couple of back up songs should He want to strip things back and create space. We have a river in Hull that is tidal and it changes direction at certain times of the day. We as worship teams must be prepared to flow with the tidal shift of the Spirit of God

I want to encourage you if you're bound by set lists and chord charts to take some time to experiment. Ask Holy Spirit to show you and guide you into this liberating place where you'll see into the heavenlies and experience his presence in a new and fresh way. Make this a part of your rehearsal time. Practice going "off piste" use the word and play the word as Holy Spirit brings you a fresh revelation. If you'll step out I promise you it will revolutionize your worship leading!

POINTS TO PONDER

- What would you say you follow the river or canal as you lead worship?

- Is your worship time predictable?

- How comfortable are you with silence in a corporate worship setting?

- What are your hopes and fears as you ponder this chapter?

I SEE A NEW FLOWER *blooming* IN THE MIDST OF THE DESERT

4

SONGS FOR THE JOURNEY

Singing as a part of our worship is one of the most beautiful ways God has given us to express our love and adoration to him. The growth of songwriters within the worship context has given us a feast of songs to choose from and we are blessed with so many different styles.

Choosing songs for our congregations to connect with, and encounter God can sometimes be a challenge depending on the musicians we have, the level of skill they carry, and the openness of our congregation to catch and receive the songs we bring to them.

It can sometimes be disheartening to listen to a song with a full band arrangement on a CD when it's you and a guitar or keyboard and that's it!

However it's worth remembering that every song usually starts out on a guitar or piano. The writer may hear the arrangement in their head but it's usually created on a solo instrument. The best songs are those that can still stand strong when they are stripped back to a single instrument and voice.

When trying these "big" songs look at ways you can adjust them for your set up. Make sure you stay true to your identity and not that of the mega church it came from.

When we choose songs we should keep in mind that we are taking our church on a journey and be careful about key choices. So many songs have big jumps from verse to chorus that if pitched wrongly, rather than helping our church family to worship, we can leave them behind. We must remember that justbecause we can sing it in that key or lower/upper octave doesn't mean they can. Our goal should be to partake at the table together not have them watch us whilst we eat!

The Bible gives us a beautiful blue print in Psalm 100:4. We are to:

ENTER HIS GATES WITH THANKSGIVING

These are the "launch" songs. They take our eyes off ourselves and focus our vision on God. We remember his goodness and faithfulness, we sing about his victory, his sacrifice, his overcoming the grave and we acknowledge all he is and all he's done. We often get this part mixed up with the sacrifice of praise. We're reminding our souls as in Psalm 43 of all the good things God has done. When we remember his faithfulness those things that weigh us down are seen from a very different perspective. I love flying and taking off. It always gives me a thrill! As we build up speed and climb higher the earth and everything it contains falls away for a time. It gets smaller and our perspective changes. So it is in this, like the runway is the first part of our worship journey. Songs that work well are Lion and the Lamb, Happy Day, Beautiful

ENTER HIS COURTS WITH PRAISE

We enter His courts with praise because that is the culture of the King that we worship. He is surrounded by praise and worship that declares His greatness and His holiness. Why a sacrifice? Well sometimes life does get in the way and even though we know the truth, our flesh can struggle to release the burdens we carry and fully enter into the praise of Jesus. There have been occasions when I have found myself in the middle of worship when my heart has been breaking in grief for the loss of a loved one or when it seems like my life is falling apart. There have been other times where I'm grappling with annoyance and I'm having an attitude about something. Truth be told I don't want to lift my hands thank you! I just want to be left to lick my wounds and growl at the injustice of my circumstances. Thankfully Holy Spirit won't allow me to stay there and He will gently remind me not of who I am, but who Jesus is. Some of my greatest encounters in praise and worship have been when I've surrendered my flesh in honour of Jesus and the truth of who He is. I'm so thankful God doesn't give up on us aren't you? One thing to remember before we move on is that praise songs aren't always up tempo songs. How great is Our God, 10,000 Reasons and Everlasting God, are great examples of slower paced praise songs.

WORSHIP

When we worship we join in with heaven. We add our voices to the angelic hosts and when we proclaim who He is He loves to show up and prove us right! I have been in meetings where people have been healed with nobody laying hands on them in any way. The power of God has swept through the room and lives have been changed. This is what I long for. To see these divine exchanges taking place, more and more.

Our worship songs need to be purely God and Jesus focussed. They are the songs that reflect what is going on in Heaven. Songs like: Worthy of it All, How Great is Our God, We Bow Down, and Revelation Song.

Worship is a place to bow down to the Lordship of Christ, to proclaim his holiness and worship who he is.

If we get this right not only is Christ glorified but hearts that are cold or far away from Him are convicted and the revelation of the kindness of God will lead to repentance. We need to be very mindful of doing too many I and me songs. I strongly believe in testifying to God's goodness in our lives but some of these songs are actually not for corporate worship but for personal times with Jesus. I want to acknowledge where I've come from, how He's delivered me and where I am now. However, I don't want to revisit too often the verses about how bad my life was before Jesus rescued me! Once we've built faith in our people we don't need to take them back to the wilderness. As a good friend expressed it's like doing a worship Hokey Cokey we're in and out of the inner court focussing on Jesus, we've ascended the mountain and are ready to fly! When choosing songs for your meeting be mindful of using too many of these type of songs too. I'd much rather sing about who He is and what He does than me! He is far more interesting!

One of the most under used type of songs in our meetings, especially our prayer meetings is that of the lament! Worship leader Michael Card calls it the lost language of worship. The Psalms are full of lament. David would often sing of his circumstances in a real and raw way but he didn't stay there. He would always declare who his God was and would always end up praising his Lord! Our worship must be real and authentic as we've previously seen. By acknowledging our weakness and the strength of our God we come into a powerful agreement with heaven that will cause a shift to take place. This excerpt from Godfrey Birtill's song Still God is a wonderful example of this.

"Where o where is Your presence oh God? In a dry and weary land?
So many people drifting away, how they need to understand
You're still God, even when we're unbelieving
Still God, when we're desperate for our healing
Still God, still God, still God
You're still God, even when our friends desert us
Still God, even through the things that hurt us
Still God, still God
So I will be still and know You are God"

We can use songs to build faith in the people we are leading. People come from all backgrounds and circumstances and we can help to lift them above those circumstances by putting songs of faith in their mouths and helping them to declare over their situations. This is why theology is so important when we write songs and when we select them. Always check as sometimes the desire to articulate in a creative way can lead to us not quite singing the truth of the word. This is our compass that directs us to worship in the full truth that sets us free!

PRAYER SONGS

The birth of the 24/7 prayer movement has brought with it some incredibly anointed songs. These songs have been written out of spontaneous times of worship and usually have a prophetic edge to them. They declare and decree the word of God over people, towns, cities, regions and nations.
They are the heaven to earth songs. Spirit Break Out, Holy Spirit You Are Welcome Here, and Shekinah Glory are wonderful examples of these songs. We should be prepared to use them in corporate worship meetings if led by Holy Spirit to intercede for something or someone. It's wise to be prepared.

There is also the prophetic song but we will look at that in another chapter.

POINTS TO PONDER

• Share about a time you've been lifted from a difficult place in worship by a song

• What do you think God wants to say to your church and community?

• Do you reflect that in the songs that you use?

• Pick one of David's Lament Psalms and work together to re write it with an emphasis on your city and region.

It's time for your resurrection, that which you thought was dead is gonna live again

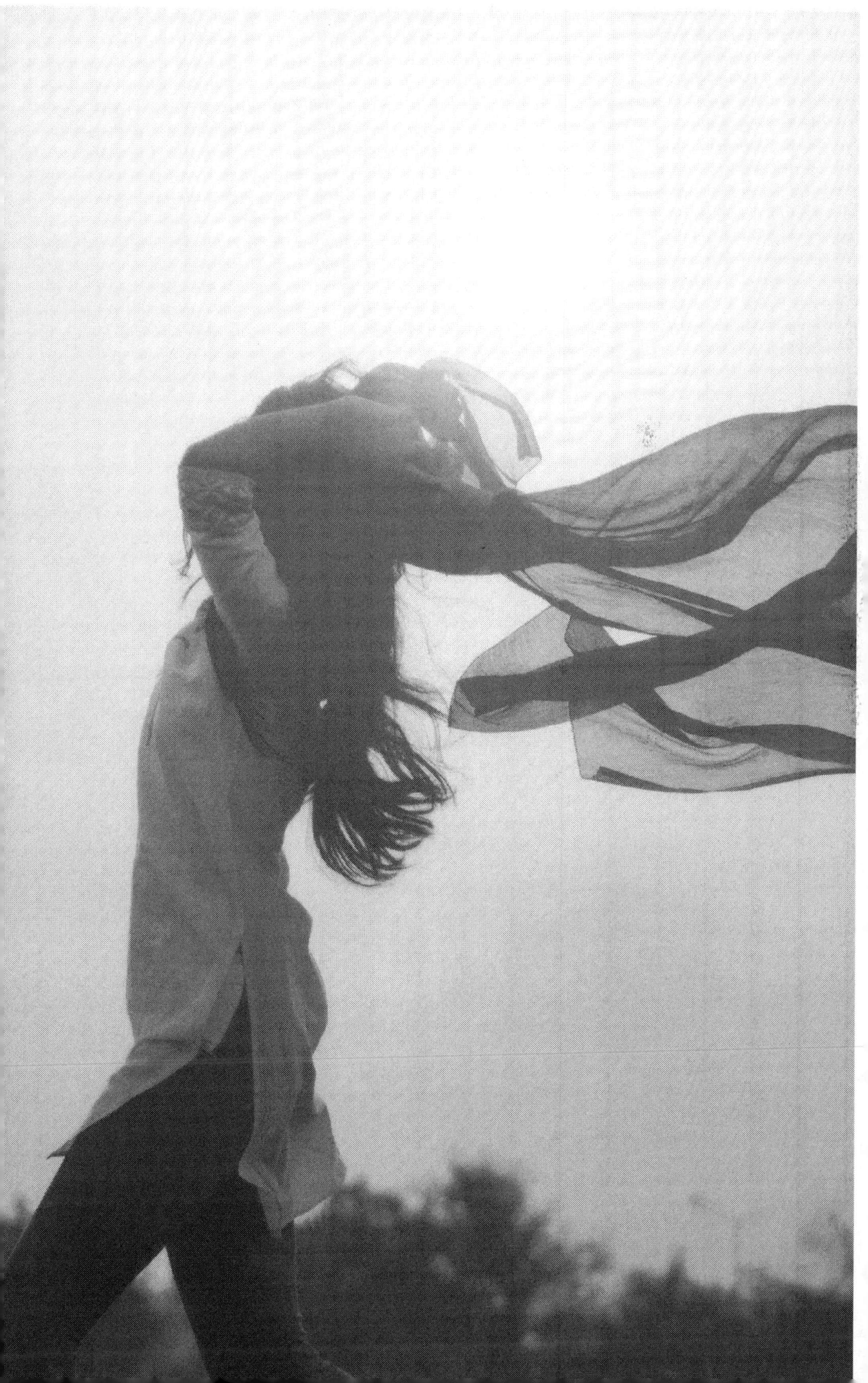

5
THE PROPHETIC SONG

In 2012 my church held our first conference in the City Hall in Hull with an evangelist called Nathan Morris. We were well into the worship when there was a pivotal moment where the congregation took over and I remember Nathan turning to myself and Paul Hemingway with a big grin and saying "you're redundant now!" it was one of the most incredible "red letter days" of my worship ministry. It impacted me greatly as hundreds sang their song and made prophetic declarations with the song that Holy Spirit released into them! The presence of God was tangible and He released his signs and wonders all over that room. Even the venue staff were impacted having never experienced anything like it before!

There is no greater place to get to in worship than the place where the congregation take over and release their song like this. We were created by God to worship so it stands to reason that He created a song for our spirit and our hearts to sing.

When couples get married they usually choose a song that is special to them for their first dance. It might be a song they heard on their first date, or perhaps when he proposed. Whatever the reason that song will be theirs and as the years go by they will look back and relate it to the love they have for each other. So it is with the song God has given us. We've become so immersed in worship "culture" that for so many that expression of worship has been buried or locked away.

I believe we are in a time where God is drawing us into a deeper place of worship where we can rediscover that song.

Isaiah sang many songs to the Lord. The song of the beloved and his vineyard Isaiah 5:1, the new song Isaiah 42:10 the song of salvation Isaiah 52:7. But perhaps the greatest worship singer ever was David who God said was "a man after His own heart" David knew what it was to release his songs to the lord. Songs of victory, songs of love, songs of lament (where are those in our repertoire??) songs of worship.

I'm blessed to travel and teach a reasonable amount and the wonder of seeing people discover the song they were born to sing never grows old. It's as though a light comes on and everything lines up. Their hearts, their spirit, their minds and their mouths!

Consider for a moment. That your sound has a frequency DNA that is linked to the church you're rooted in and those in your community? What would happen if we embarked on a journey to restore this song and the church started to worship more with this, than those on the computer screen?

We have a dog who likes the sound of her own voice. She is convinced she is there to guard the whole street. As noble as this is it can be annoying when she barks. Wanting to find a solution I did what all internet scholars do I Googled it! I found a device that when a button was pressed emitted a very high frequency sound that only a dogs ears are tuned to. The idea is that it distracts them enough to forget why they are barking and eventually they stop. It changes their behaviour. I am led to wonder whether the people in our communities are wired to respond to the worship frequency in our churches in a similar way.

There is a frequency that God has placed in them that matches ours. Paul and Silas understood this when they released their worship songs unto the Lord. We know the story. An earthquake strikes, the doors fly open and ALL the prisoners are released. Now that in itself is amazing but it goes a step further when the guard realizing what had happened called out to Paul and Silas and asked "what must I do to be saved?" We know that his whole family came to know the Lord.

I'm not suggesting a Pied Piper theory but I do believe when we are authentic in our worship and are genuinely led by Holy Spirit and trust Him to release that which He has placed within us we will see amazing things!

Fear is the biggest thief that stops us releasing our song. The devil knows the impact it will have and does his best to make us fearful and insecure which can lead to us living under a spirit of rejection.

Have you ever been in a situation where Holy Spirit has asked you to step out of your comfort zone and do something new? Your mouth dries up, your palms get sweaty, your stomach rolls like a stormy ocean and your heart feels like it's going to beat its way right out of your chest! We sweat, we argue with ourselves saying it's not God it's just our flesh and we make every excuse not to obey. This is what fear does. There's a battle for your voice that is raging around you every time you open your mouth to praise.

I remember being in a meeting where I had been invited to speak. During the worship I had a picture of hands around my throat constricting my vocal chords and another where the same hands were clamped over my mouth. I asked the Lord about it and He told me it was a picture of some people in The Church that had been silenced by fear.

It's time to face down the fear, look it right in the eyes and see it for what it is. It's like the Wizard of Oz who hid behind the big curtain using a machine to magnify His voice and therefore scare everyone who ever encountered him! The devil is a liar and will never tell you the truth. Decide today who you're going to believe and move from captivity to freedom. Release your song and let the other captives hear it and be freed also!!

Now I know some of you are reading this and thinking I can't sing Angie. I've been told to put my fist in my mouth and be quiet. I'm a musician not a singer! Well, I am convinced Gods ears aren't tuned in the same way that ours are. I also read in my bible that He says to make a joyful NOISE unto the Lord. Yes we sing a new song but I think He's interested in every voice whether it be like that of an angel or otherwise. You have to know He takes delight in the sound you're releasing but even more in you who is releasing the sound!

My friend is a wonderful worshipper who is completely tone deaf! Does she care? Heck no! She sings with great gusto and worships like it's her last day on earth and her first in heaven! I envy her, her freedom and passion to give everything to the Lord in sung worship.It's not just about the sung word. As an instrumentalist you can play prophetically too. There is a melody and a chord structure that God wants to release to you that will minister to people just like David did to Saul!

So today let's break our covenant with insecurity and fear of rejection and move into the place of pure worship. Spend time with God in your private place and practice singing your song. Connectyour spirit to your mouth and release it from there. Not your brain where you are affected by how you feel but from your spirit. When you sing from your spirit that is connected to God's Spirit your brain, your heart and your emotions will line up!

Releasing the song of the Lord can seem like a daunting thing but Zephaniah 3:17 tells us "the Lord your God is with you, the Mighty Warrior who saves. He will take great delight in you; in His love He will no longer rebuke you, but will rejoice over you with singing." There is delight and joy in the song He sings over us! It is a song of affirmation and encouragement as all prophecy is.

We have entered into a season where the prophetic is being awakened in the church and there is a need for worship teams to grasp and catch the season we are in. There is a window open over us where God is pouring out words and songs and a new level of creativity within the worship context like we've never seen before.

On a missions trip to Albania I was asked to play piano in a meeting. I've been leading worship for over 20 years but I'd only recently started leading on piano. To say I was scared was an understatement as I squeaked my way through a song! However after a few verses I clearly heard Holy Spirit say "Angie ditch the song and let me hear yours!" with that I launched into my own worship and I knew I'd dropped notes and hit a couple of wrong ones but it was as if He had stepped in and "fixed" my mistakes! I learned a valuable lesson in trusting the anointing that God pours out that day!

Luke 6:45 tells us that "out of the heart the mouth speaks" God is placing a passion for souls in the heart, He is placing a passion for healing and a passion for orphans and social justice in the hearts of you and I. When our hearts are filled with an understanding and acceptance of His love for us we can release that revelation in a song that will impact others. I've often found myself singing about God's love in a small gathering and seen people weep like children because they realise just how precious they are to Him and it breaks all insecurity and brings healing and freedom!

Work together as a team and practice this. Practice without music first, learn to hear for each other, build relationship, for this is the foundation for moving in the supernatural and the prophetic within the worship team. I've been amazed at how musicians I've worked with out of relationship have had this amazing sense of knowing exactly what I want to do and where I want to go without me even saying a word.
I cannot stress enough the importance of investing in each other relationally! It's not enough to play instruments, sing and be driven by serving. Jesus was all

about relationship and developed his team of disciples over meals as much as he did performing miracles! Developing in prophetic worship away from the public arena of meetings will take you to greater levels of gifting and will be far more enjoyable than trying it in front of your congregation.

POINTS TO PONDER

- What stops you from releasing a prophetic song or sound?

- How can you as a team grow together in relationship?

- What do you dream of seeing when you minister in worship?

- What steps can you take to see this happen?

Be still and know that I am God

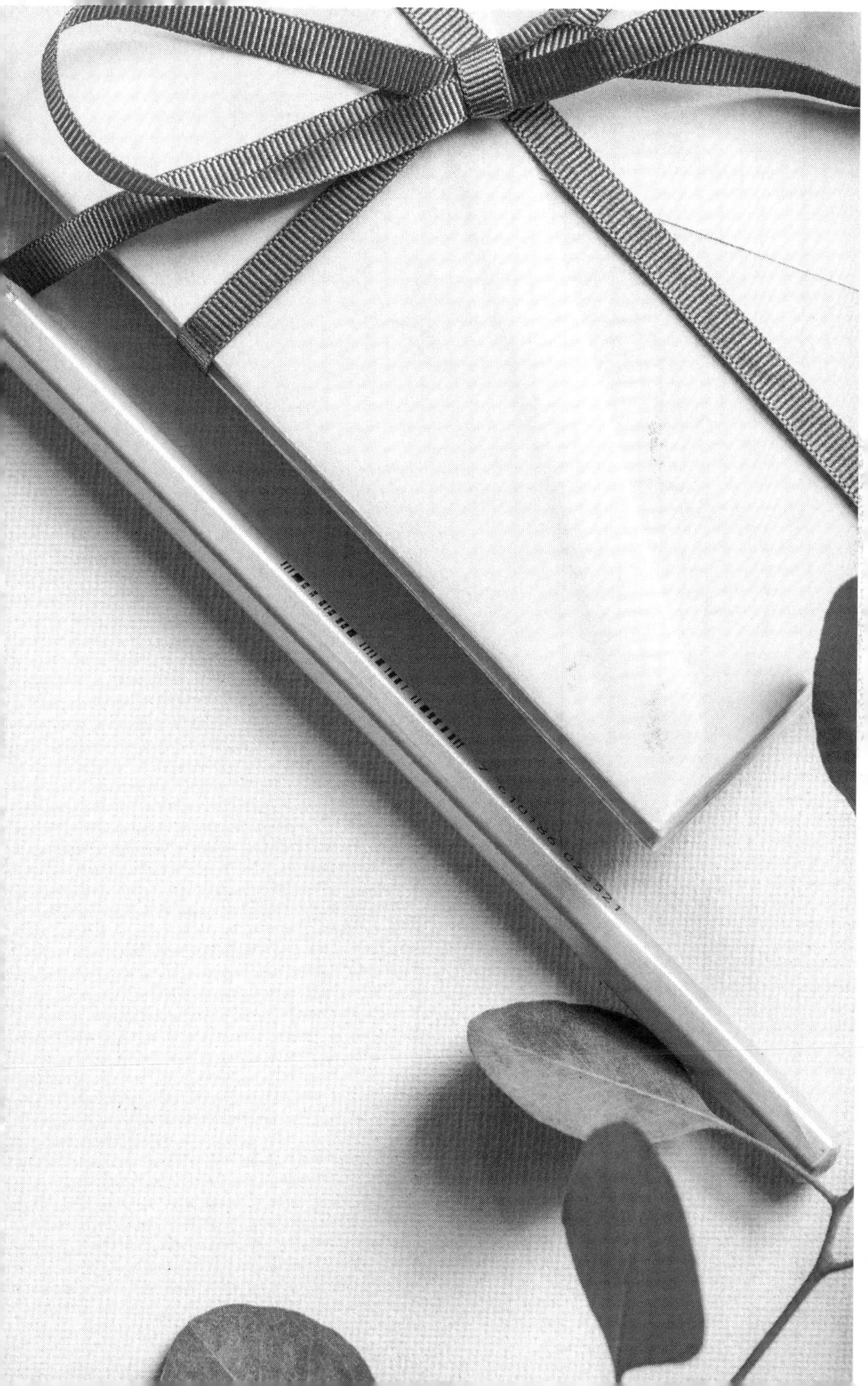

6

DEAR FRIEND

I'm so glad you're reading this because it means you have come to the end of my first book and have stuck with it. I wanted to share with you a little bit about my journey before we part ways for a while, so please allow me to share a very significant part of my life and ministry with you. It is my hope that this will help you to remain healthy in spirit, body and mind.

I remember the day God called me into worship ministry. We'd just visited our local Christian book shop and we'd purchased a Hillsong CD. The very first chord sounded and the beautiful anointed voice of Darlene Zschech filled that car and something leapt in my spirit. I knew what I was called to do. The memory of that experience moves me even as I'm writing this.

I liken it to John the Baptist leaping in His mother's womb when he heard the voice of the woman who was carrying the one he would serve in later years.

The very destiny God had placed in me at my spiritual conception was being awakened and brought to birth. I started to pray asking the Lord to show me a sign if this was Him. I eagerly awaited His response.

I was so excited but I didn't have a clue and doubted it was God, believing He would want me to be a missionary to Africa or somewhere. He, however, was not phased and went to great lengths to confirm His call on my life. A few weeks later I was pushing my trolley around our local supermarket when a song came on the overhead speaker. It was a song I hadn't heard in a while. I was trying to connect where I'd heard it when I suddenly realised through the noise of the other shoppers that it was me singing! This was a song I had recorded some 12 years previously for a company that supplied stores with music. It was an original song written by a friend. The name of the song was called "Let's Start it All Again!" I knew this was God. These songs never made it past a month in circulation never mind 12 years! I never heard that song again. God had spoken His Rhema word!

I then started to ask the Lord to show me step by step what to do next. Later on that month I was at an event and received a prophetic word that God had heard my prayers and would show me step by step the way forward! I wept at the enormity of His love for me. I read every book on worship I could find, I listened to CD's and I dreamed of being used by God to bring peace, healing and freedom to people through my worship.

I joined our small church worship team and immersed myself in His presence as much as I could. Whenever I read those books there was one theme that always came through. It was that of ALWAYS putting Jesus first. To seek first His kingdom and His righteousness before anything else.

Now I'm a Martha in the flesh but a Mary in the spirit! This has caused me no end of tension. Years went on and I had some amazing opportunities to travel in ministry, I was in leadership in my local church and from outward appearances it was all going very well. But on the inside it was a very different story! I was weary, I was burned out and Jesus felt a million miles away. I knew that I should have rested more and be still and yet my hands always seemed to find something to do! I'd lost my confidence comparing myself to others and was now performing a ritual rather than ministering. I was afraid of letting people down and so continued with the scenario until God rescued me and made me "lay down in green pastures" for a good while.

I cannot honestly remember a time where my heart has felt so smashed. It looked hopeless and I wasn't sure I'd recover. But my God is really amazing at resurrection! He can take the most broken and burned out life and breathe His life back into it.

There followed a time of going back to basics and re discovering who Jesus said that I am, and finding my identity in Him! Eventually the day came where He released me to take up ministry again and this time it was with a very different attitude.

I tell you this because this is the greatest danger we face when we enter into any form of ministry. It's not envy or arrogance that we are enticed into but that of being driven and doing/serving without the appropriate rest and relationship with Jesus. The devil knows that if he can burn us out we will withdraw from friendships, accountability and we will get disillusioned and weary of doing good. It's a very subtle journey into that place. We have to be aware of how we're doing and brave enough to share with a trusted friend when we're out of alignment so they can help us to get back to a healthy place. We know the enemy will do anything he can to attack worship ministries. We don't give him any glory by dwelling on this but to be forewarned is to be forearmed. We do have an enemy who comes to seek, kill and destroy.

So my friend please learn from my experience. Always make time to be with the one who sees the gold in you and wants to have you minister that gift He's placed within you to Him first. It's not that He needs it but rather that He wants it. He wants to hear your voice because it moves His heart and brings Him joy. We weren't created to minister, we were created to walk with Him in the cool of the day. He is jealous for us because He created us for relationship with Him and Him alone. Yes He placed gifts in you at your conception but they were first and foremost for Him. Let Him fill your heart with His presence and love and all the other treasure that He wants to put in there and then minister from that overflow.

I know He has good plans for you and you will go on to do amazing things for Him but remember the greatest platform is that of your life every day not just two hours on a Sunday morning.

So keep seeking His kingdom and His heart and ALL these other things like worship leading, singing, and playing your instrument will be added to this and you will soar!

Much Love

Angie